A New True Book

THE GREAT LAKES

By Kathy Henderson

CHILDRENS PRESS ®
CHICAGO

Split Rock Lighthouse
on Lake Superior

Library of Congress Cataloging-in-Publication Data

Henderson, Kathy, 1949-
   The Great Lakes / by Kathy Henderson.
      p.   cm.—(A New true book)
   Includes index.
   Summary: An introduction to the five fresh-water lakes that contain one-fifth of the earth's standing fresh water.
   ISBN 0-516-01163-4
   1.   Great Lakes—Juvenile literature.
[1.   Great Lakes.]   I.   Title.
GB1627.G8H46   1989   88-34670
551.48'2'0977—dc19   CIP
                                       AC

TABLE OF CONTENTS

FRESH WATER OCEANS

The Atlantic Ocean borders the east coast of North America. The Pacific Ocean lies along the west coast. Both of these huge oceans are filled with salt water.

Canada and the United States are in North America. They share these salt water oceans and another very different coast. This coast is

Opposite page: Seagulls hunt for food on the Great Lakes.

Lake Huron

sometimes called the
"third coast." It surrounds
five freshwater lakes
known as the Great Lakes.
Some of the Great
Lakes are so large that

6

early explorers thought they were oceans. Now geologists believe that the Great Lakes may have been part of the Atlantic Ocean millions of years ago. Fossilized bones from whales and other creatures that live in the ocean have been found in the lake areas.

Eight states and one Canadian province border the Great Lakes. The lakes themselves cover more

than 95,000 square miles, an area larger than the states of Pennsylvania and New York combined.

The five lakes and their connecting waterways stretch 2,342 miles from Kingston, Ontario, at the eastern tip of Lake Ontario to Duluth, Minnesota, at the western edge of Lake Superior. In between are Lake Erie, Lake Huron, and Lake Michigan.

MINNESOTA

CANADA, PROVINCE OF ONTARIO

Lake Superior

Duluth

MICHIGAN

St. Marys River

Lake Huron

Straits of Mackinac

Kingston

WISCONSIN

Lake Michigan

Toronto

Lake Ontario

IOWA

MICHIGAN

St. Clair River

ILLINOIS

Detroit River

Lake Erie

INDIANA

OHIO

PENNSYLVANIA

Lake Michigan is the only lake completely within the borders of the United States. Lake Superior is the largest freshwater lake in the entire world. It is also the coldest and

9

Mackinac Bridge is one of the world's longest suspension bridges. The bridge crosses the Straits of Mackinac.

deepest of the Great Lakes. Lake Ontario is the smallest of the Great Lakes, and Lake Erie is the shallowest.

Lake Huron is the only lake that connects to more than one Great Lake. The

St. Marys River

Detroit and St. Clair rivers connect it to Lake Erie. The Straits of Mackinac connect Lake Huron to Lake Michigan. The St. Marys River connects Lake Huron to Lake Superior.

Altogether, the Great
Lakes contain one-fifth of
the earth's standing fresh
water. Now you know why
explorers thought they
were looking at oceans!

HOW THE LAKES WERE FORMED

Compared with the earth's age, the Great Lakes are just babies. Like children, they grew and changed over the last two billion years.

Much of the rock and sediment around and under the Great Lakes was formed billions of years ago. Later huge sheets of glacial ice, which also contained heavy rocks,

Rocky shore of Lake Huron (right) and palisades along Lake Superior (opposite page)

spread over the land. In some areas, the weight of the rocks and ice caused the land to sink, or depress.

When the climate
became warmer, the
glacial ice melted. The
water drained into the deep
grooves that cut through
the land. These became
rivers. Some water was
trapped in the depressions.
This was the beginning of
the Great Lakes.

Over millions of years,
glacial ice spread and
melted many times. Each
time the shape and size of

Lake Superior Provincial Park, Ontario, Canada

the young lakes changed.
The last major change to
the Great Lakes occurred
about 3,500 years ago.

Ancient Ojibway rock painting (above)
and Chippewa wigwam (right)

INDIANS AND EXPLORERS

Indian tribes lived near
the Great Lakes for
thousands of years. They
had learned to use the
waterways for food and
travel long before the first
foreigners came to explore
the New World.

In the mid-1300s, the Vikings were the first white men to come. An inscription on a large stone in Minnesota tells of their travels.

Runestone Monument in Alexandria, Minnesota

Jacques Cartier (inset) explored the St. Lawrence River and met with the tribes.

Over one hundred years
went by before more
explorers came. Jacques
Cartier, a Frenchman,
sailed across the Atlantic
and partway up the St.
Lawrence River in 1535.

Samuel de Champlain also explored for France.

He claimed the area for France. Soon other explorers, such as Samuel de Champlain, Étienne Brulé, and Jean Nicolet, followed.

The explorers traveled north and west across the

land and inland waterways. They were searching for a water route to the rich trade in China and Japan. Instead they found many Indian tribes and enormous herds of animals that were prized for their fur coats. They also discovered the Great Lakes.

Lake Huron was the first to be discovered by the explorers as they moved farther west. Then Lake Superior was found, and finally Lake Michigan.

DuSable built the first cabin in Chicago (above) not far from the shores of Lake Michigan. At first, the Indians (left) welcomed the explorers. Frequently, the rough waters of the Great Lakes proved more dangerous than the Indians.

It was several years later before explorers traveled south and found Lake Ontario. Lake Erie was the last to be explored. It had been carefully guarded by the Iroquois Indians.

French missionaries soon came to the Great Lakes. They tried to teach the Indians Christian ways.

A Jesuit missionary preaches to the Indians.

Forts and missions were
built at various ports
around the lakes. Eventually,
British explorers, fur traders,
and lumbermen also
came to the area.

Fort Howard on Green Bay as it looked in 1838 (above).
Reconstruction of Old Fort William in Canada (below).

SAILING THE GREAT LAKES

More and more Europeans came to settle around the Great Lakes. They fished. They built towns and cities. They started lumber mills. They mined for copper and iron ore. Other businesses followed. Soon hundreds of ships carrying passengers and cargo sailed the Great Lakes.

The first ship to sail on

the Great Lakes was the *Griffin* in 1679. It was built on Lake Erie and sailed all the way to Green Bay, Wisconsin. There the crew loaded it with furs and set sail for Montreal. On the way back it disappeared. No one knows what happened to the ship or its crew.

Sailors soon learned that sailing the Great Lakes was more dangerous than sailing the oceans. Specially designed ships were built.

A whaleback freighter

A whaleback freighter
was one such special ship.
The top looked like a
regular freighter but the
bottom was rounded like a
submarine's. Some people
called them "pig boats"
because of their funny
snub-nosed bows.

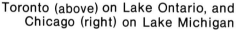
Toronto (above) on Lake Ontario, and
Chicago (right) on Lake Michigan

Today, few people travel
the Great Lakes by ship
except in pleasure boats.
But hundreds of freighters
still carry tons of cargo
back and forth across the
Great Lakes.

Sailboats and freighters
sail the Great Lakes
when weather permits.

The Erie Canal was
begun in 1817. A series
of locks (above left) and canals
connected the Hudson River with
Lake Erie. Opened in 1825, the
Erie Canal was a great success.

CANALS AND LOCKS

Over the years, many canals and locks have been built to connect the Great Lakes. They allow ships to bypass river rapids, waterfalls, and shallow water so that a ship can travel from the Atlantic Ocean to all the ports on the Great Lakes.

The Erie Canal was one of the first of these man-made waterways to be

Niagara
Falls

built. It is 363 miles long
and took years to build.
The Erie Canal bypasses
the St. Lawrence River
between Buffalo and
Albany, New York.

The Welland Canal helps
ships go around Niagara

Falls. It has forty locks that raise or lower ships the 326-foot distance in height between Lake Ontario and Lake Erie.

The Soo Locks, located between the upper

The Soo Locks connect Lake Superior and Lake Huron.

peninsula of Michigan and Canada, allow ships to travel between Lake Superior and Lake Huron. In 1959 the St. Lawrence Seaway opened.

St. Lambert Lock on the St. Lawrence River is part of the seaway system.

It was built by the United States and Canada. The Seaway system provided a waterway deep enough and safe enough for most ocean freighters to sail

Edison-Sault hydroelectric power plant at Sault St. Marie, Michigan

into the Great Lakes
directly from the Atlantic
Ocean.

In addition to canals, the
Seaway provided dams
and power-making plants
to make electricity for New
York, Vermont, and Ontario.

FUTURE OF THE GREAT LAKES

Ecologists worry about the future of the Great Lakes. Over the years, the lakes have become dangerously polluted. Many types of fish and other water creatures have died off.

People have polluted the Great Lakes with human and chemical wastes.

Steel mills on the shores of Lake Michigan

Beaches have sometimes been closed.

Some pollution has occurred naturally. But much of the pollution has been caused by toxic chemicals that many industries have dumped into the Great Lakes.

Many people are now working together to clean up the Great Lakes and save them from further pollution. The lakes have been restocked with fish.

Efforts to clean up the Great Lakes and restock them with fish have been successful.

People enjoy
clean beaches.

Beaches have been re-
opened. New laws have
been passed to regulate
the dumping of toxic
chemicals.

Grain elevators (left), ship docks (middle), and rail yards (below), have been built along the Great Lakes.

The Great Lakes have developed into one of the busiest industrial regions in the world. Yet there

are many places along the
Great Lakes shoreline that
look the same today as
they did years ago.
Ancient rock formations

tower above clear, cold
water. And you can almost
see the Indians and
explorers paddling their
birch-bark canoes.

WORDS YOU SHOULD KNOW

cargo(KAR • go) — materials or merchandise carried in a ship, railroad car, plane, truck

claim(CLAYM) — demand as one's right to own

climate(CLY • mitt) — the usual weather in a given area

crew(CROO) — the group of persons who operate a ship, train, plane

depressions(dih • PRESH • unz) — places pushed lower down with force

foreigner(FOR • en • er) — person belonging to another country

fossils(FOSS • ulz) — ancient plant or animal remains in petrified form

geologist(gee • AHL • uh • jist) — person who studies the history of earth's development

herds(HERDZ) — groups of animals raised, traveling, or feeding together

industrial(in • DUSS • tree • uhl) — producing, manufacturing products by machinery or manual labor

locks(LOX) — series of sections filled or emptied of water as a ship needs raising or lowering to travel from one water level to another

passengers(PASS • en • jerz) — persons who travel in a vehicle

sediment(SEHD • ih • ment) — the materials that settle to the bottom of bodies of water

shallow(SHALL • low) — not deep

strait(STRAYT) — narrow waterway that joins two larger bodies of water

trade(TRAID) — exchange of goods and money

INDEX

About the Author

Kathy Henderson is Executive Director of the National Association for Young Writers, vice president of the NAYW Board of Trustees, and Michigan Adviser for the Society of Children's Book Writers. She works closely with children, teachers, and librarians through young author conferences and workshops, and is a frequent guest speaker in schools. An experienced freelance writer with hundreds of newspaper and magazine articles to her credit, she is also the author of the Market Guide for Young Writers. *Mrs. Henderson lives on a 400-acre dairy farm in Michigan with her husband Keith, and two teenage children.*